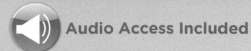

## Audio Access Included

Visit **www.halleonard.com/mylibrary**

Enter Code
1796-9242-2682-9312

# CLASSICAL THEMES
## FOR KEYBOARD PERCUSSION

## CONTENTS

Audio Arrangements by Peter Deneff
Tracking, mixing, and mastering by BeatHouse Music

ISBN 978-1-4803-6057-0

7777 W. BLUEMOUND RD. P.O. BOX 13819 MILWAUKEE, WI 53213

In Australia Contact:
**Hal Leonard Australia Pty. Ltd.**
4 Lentara Court
Cheltenham, Victoria, 3192 Australia
Email: ausadmin@halleonard.com.au

Visit Hal Leonard Online at
**www.halleonard.com**

# FINLANDIA

By JEAN SIBELIUS

# MORNING
from PEER GYNT

By EDVARD GRIEG

# SYMPHONY NO. 1
## Fourth Movement Excerpt

By JOHANNES BRAHMS

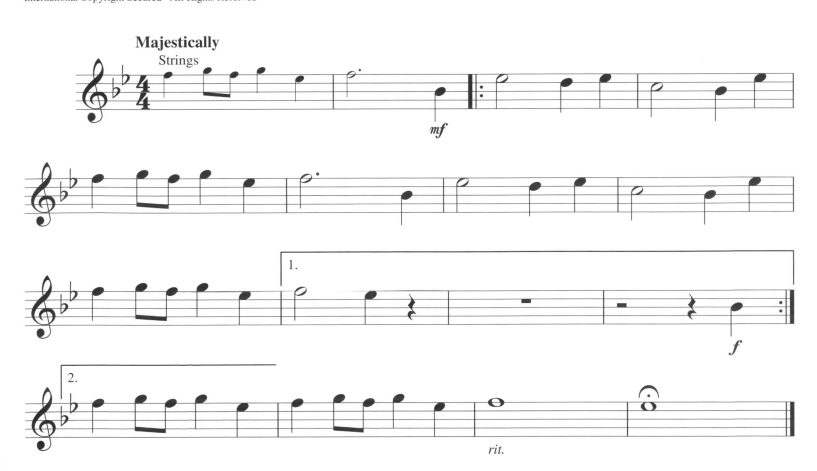

# CARNIVAL OF VENICE

By JULIUS BENEDICT

# SPRING
## from THE FOUR SEASONS

By ANTONIO VIVALDI

# CAN CAN
from ORPHEUS IN THE UNDERWORLD

By JACQUES OFFENBACH

# MUSETTE
from THE ANNA MAGDALENA NOTEBOOK

By JOHANN SEBASTIAN BACH

# TRUMPET VOLUNTARY
### (Prince of Denmark's March)

By JEREMIAH CLARKE

# LARGO
from SYMPHONY NO. 9 ("New World")

By ANTONIN DVOŘÁK

# ODE TO JOY
from SYMPHONY NO. 9

By LUDWIG VAN BEETHOVEN

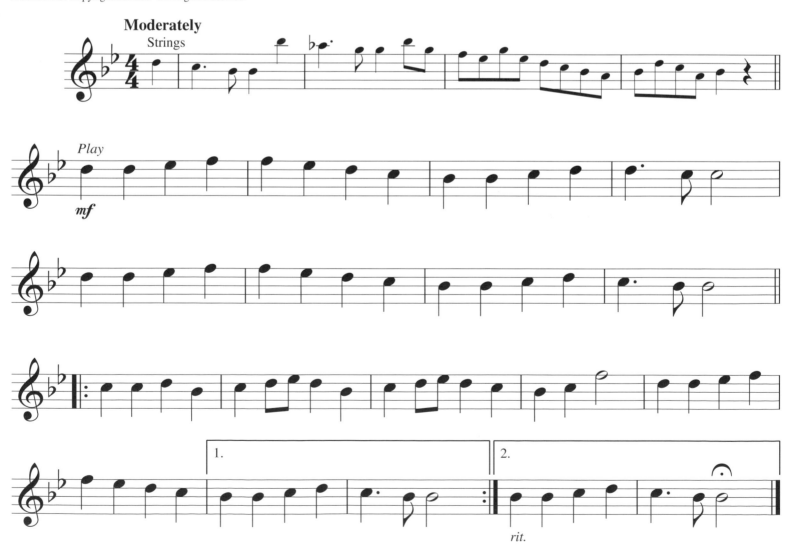